Amazon Echo Dot

––––– ❧❧❧❧ –––––

The ultimate Amazon Echo Dot user guide and manual

Table of Contents

Introduction

Thank you for taking the time to read this user guide for the Amazon Echo Dot!

This book serves as a complete user guide for the Echo Dot, and will teach you all you need to know about using this amazing device!

You will soon learn how to setup your Echo Dot, the different things you can use it for, the different commands you can use, and how to download and install new Skills to your Echo Dot device!

At the completion of this book you should be confident in using your Echo Dot for a wide variety of tasks!

If you come across any issues when using your Echo Dot, this book also contains a troubleshooting section at the back to assist you.

Once again, thanks for pickup up this book! I hope you find it to be helpful, and enjoy using your Echo Dot!

Chapter 1:

Overview of
the Amazon Echo Dot

So what is the Echo Dot?

The Echo Dot is a small, roughly hockey puck sized device that will allow you to access Amazon's voice enabled personal assistant, Alexa. Alexa is a smart personal assistant and can be used to do anything from adding events to your calendar to ordering an Uber! One of Alexa's main functions is the ability to control music playback using your voice. The Echo Dot includes a small, built-in speaker so Alexa can speak to you. If you wish to use your Echo Dot for music playback, you'll need to hook up a set of speakers. If you already have an audio system you love, the Echo Dot is a great option to allow you to control your music playback via voice commands.

The Echo Dot can also be used to control smart home devices. There's a large list of compatible smart devices already, and more are being added every day! If you're looking to make your home smart, you can buy 6 and 12 packs of Echo Dots and add one to each room of your house so you can access Alexa from anywhere. Alexa is smart, and will only respond to your questions or commands on the closest device!

The Echo Dot is currently available in both black and white, and a variety of decals are available to personalize your device to fit your décor. You'll be sure to find something that suits your personal style!

So how does Alexa work?

The "brains" of Alexa aren't actually in your Echo Dot, they're stored online in the cloud. When you give Alexa a command or ask her a question, Alexa records your voice and sends your request online to Amazon's "Alexa Voice Services". Amazon uses voice recognition to determine what you've said to Alexa, and then analyses your query to work out what Alexa should do. Amazon then sends a response back to your Echo Dot with the answer to your request. For example, if you asked Alexa "What is the weather like in New York today?" here's what would happen:

- A recording of your question would be sent online to Amazon

- Voice recognition would determine what you've said and convert it to text

- Natural language processing would be used to determine the meaning of your question

- Amazon finds the current weather forecast for New York

- A response is sent back to your Echo Dot and Alexa tells you the forecast

All of this should happen seamlessly and in the space of a few seconds as if you were having a regular conversation with a person. We'll cover some basic commands and good questions to ask Alexa in chapter 4.

You may be wondering how Alexa knows when you're talking to her. Your Echo Dot has 7 built-in microphones and is always listening for you to give Alexa a command. Your Echo Dot will know you're talking to Alexa if you say the "wake-word". By default, the wake-word is "Alexa", but you can change this to "Echo" or "Amazon" if you prefer.

You may be worried that everything you say is being recorded by your Echo Dot and sent to Amazon. This is not the case. Even though it's always listening, your Echo Dot will only start sending data to Amazon when it hears the wake-word. If you don't want your Echo Dot to continually listen for the wake-word, you can temporarily mute your microphones. If you do this, you'll need to unmute your Echo Dot to be able to talk to Alexa.

Some of the commands you say to Alexa are recorded and stored on your device. This is not designed to track what you're asking Alexa, but is there to improve Alexa's recognition of your voice and speech patterns and make her more accurate. If you have privacy concerns, we'll cover how to mute your Echo Dot and delete any recordings later on in the book.

Chapter 2:

Setting up your Echo Dot

In this chapter we will cover how to setup your Echo Dot so that it's ready to use!

To setup your Echo Dot you will need:

- A Wi-Fi connection

- An Echo Dot

- A phone or tablet running Fire OS 3.0 or higher, Android 4.4 or higher, or iOS 8.0 or higher OR a Wi-Fi enabled computer

Step One: Download the Alexa app

Download the Alexa app from the Apple app store, Google Play or the Amazon app store. Once the app has finished downloading, please sign in to your Amazon account.

If you are using a computer to setup Alexa, browse to https://alexa.amazon.com on your computer using Safari, Chrome, Firefox, Microsoft Edge, or Internet Explorer, and then login to your Amazon account.

Step Two: Power on your device

Plug in your Echo Dot and turn it on. The light ring on your Echo Dot should turn blue and then orange, and then Alexa will greet you. Your Echo Dot is now in setup mode.

Step Three: Connect your Echo Dot to Wi-Fi.

- In the Alexa app or on your computer, open the navigation panel on the left side of the screen and select "Settings" then "Set up a new device".

- Press and hold the Action button on your Echo Dot until the light ring turns orange. A list of Wi-Fi networks should now appear in the Alexa app.

- Select your Wi-Fi network and enter your password. If you are planning on setting up more than one Echo Dot on your network, select the option to "Save your Wi-Fi password to Amazon". This will make setup faster on your other devices.

- Select "Connect" and your Echo Dot will now connect to the Wi-Fi network.

Step Four: Voice Training

This step is optional, but it will improve Alexa's voice recognition accuracy. Within the Alexa app select "Settings" and then "Voice Training". Alexa will now have you repeat some phrases to improve her voice recognition. Ideally, you should repeat this process with everyone who will be using your Echo Dot so that Alexa can become familiar with their voices.

Step Five: Customize your experience

Now is a good opportunity to add some details to your Alexa app to customize your experience. At the very least, you should set your device location so that time and weather information are accurate and Alexa can find local business information.

To set the device location:

- In the Alexa app, open the left navigation panel, and then select "Settings".

- Select your Echo Dot from the list.

- In the Device location section, select "Edit".

- Enter your complete address, including the street name, city, state, and ZIP code.

- Select "Save".

Other details you may want to add are your preferred news sources, favorite sports teams, commute details, and Google calendar accounts. You can change these settings by selecting "Settings" and then "Account" within the Alexa app. These details are used to provide you with customized answers when asking Alexa for the news, sports scores, and traffic conditions, or when adding items to your calendar or to-do list.

Chapter 3:

Adding External speakers and the Alexa voice remote

You have two different options for connecting speakers to your Echo Dot. You can either use a 3.5mm audio cable to connect your speakers or you can connect via Bluetooth. Both options are quick and easy to set up, so it's up to personal preference which you would prefer. Keep in mind that your Echo Dot can only connect to one Bluetooth device at a time so if you want to playback music from your phone you should connect your speakers via audio cable.

Setup via audio cable:

1. Place your Echo Dot and your speakers at least 3 feet apart. Alexa won't be able to hear you clearly if your speakers are too close to the microphones of your Echo Dot!

2. Power your speakers on and turn the volume up.

3. Plug one end of a 3.5mm audio cable into your Echo Dot and the other end into your speakers. If your speakers don't have a 3.5mm audio port you can buy an adapter to allow you to plug your speakers in.

That's it! You should now be able to play audio from your Echo Dot through your speakers.

Setup via Bluetooth:

1. Place your Echo Dot and your speakers at least 3 feet apart. Alexa won't be able to hear you clearly if your speakers are too close to the microphones of your Echo Dot!

2. Power your speakers on and turn the volume up.

3. Turn on Bluetooth pairing mode on your speakers. Check the user guide for your speakers if you don't know how to do this.

4. Open the Alexa app and select "Settings" and then select your Echo Dot from the list.

5. Select "Bluetooth" > "Pair a new device". Your Echo Dot will now search for Bluetooth devices. When it finds your speaker it should appear in the Alexa app.

6. Select your speaker from the Bluetooth device list. Alexa will tell you pairing was successful.

7. Select "Continue". You can now play audio from your Echo Dot through your speakers.

That's it! Your speakers are all set up! If you'd like to disconnect your speakers from your Echo Dot in the future you can just say "Alexa, disconnect". You won't need to go through this whole setup process when you wish to reconnect your speakers either. You can just say "Alexa, connect" and your speakers will reconnect to your Echo Dot.

Adding the Alexa voice remote:

The Alexa voice remote is an optional accessory you can use with your Echo Dot. This remote pairs with your Echo Dot via Bluetooth and can be used to allow you to talk to Alexa when you're in a noisy room or out of range of the microphones on your Echo Dot. Just press the microphone button on the remote and speak your question and your Echo Dot will respond. To get your remote set up, first make sure you have inserted batteries and then:

1. Open the Alexa app and select "Settings"

2. Select your Echo Dot from the list and then select "Pair remote"

3. Hold down the Play/Pause button on the remote for 5 seconds. Your Echo Dot will now pair with your remote; this may take a few seconds. Alexa will let you know when your remote has successfully paired.

Chapter 4:

Basic Commands

Now that your Echo Dot is set up you can start giving Alexa some commands. Alexa has a variety of built in commands, and you can add more functionality by adding "Skills" to Alexa. For now, we're just going to cover the basics, and will talk more about adding skills later in the book. Some of the following commands require you to have customized your Alexa experience by setting your device location, commute, sports and news preferences, and linking a Google Calendar.

Universal Commands

"Alexa, help" – Alexa provides help

"Alexa, repeat" – Alexa will repeat what she last said

"Alexa, stop" – Alexa will stop the current activity, e.g. music playback

"Alexa, cancel" – Cancels the previous command

Volume Commands

"Alexa, mute" – mutes Alexa

"Alexa, unmute" – Unmutes Alexa

"Alexa, set volume to [0-10]" – Sets volume

"Alexa, louder" – Increases volume

"Alexa, turn up/down the volume" – Increases/decreases volume

"Alexa, turn up the bass" – Increases the bass

"Alexa, turn down the treble" – Decreases the treble

"Alexa, increase the midrange" – Increases the midrange

Time and date

"Alexa, set an alarm for [time]." – Sets an alarm

"Alexa, wake me up at [time] in the morning." – Sets an alarm

"Alexa, set a repeating alarm for [day] at [time]." – Sets a repeating alarm

"Alexa, when's my next alarm?" – Alexa will tell you when you next alarm is

"Alexa, cancel my alarm for 2 p.m." – Cancels alarm

"Alexa, snooze." – Snoozes alarm

"Alexa, set a timer for [##] minutes." – Sets a timer

"Alexa, how much time is left on my timer?" – Alexa returns how long is left on your timer

"Alexa, what time is it?" – Alexa tells the current time

"Alexa, what's the date?" – Alexa tells the current date

"Alexa, when is [holiday] this year?" – Alexa tells you when the holiday is

Math

"Alexa, how many [units] are in [units]?" – Converts between units

"Alexa, what's [number] plus [number]?" – Alexa can add, subtract, multiply and divide

"Alexa, [#] factorial." – Alexa can do advanced math like factorials

Dictionary

"Alexa, what's the definition of [word]?" – Alexa tells you the word definition

"Alexa, how do you spell [word]?" – Alexa tells you how to spell a word

To do/Shopping lists

"Alexa, add [task] to my to-do list" – Adds the task to your to-do list

"Alexa, add [item] to my shopping list" – Adds an item to your shopping list

"Alexa, what's on my to-do/shopping list" – Alexa tells you what's on your list

"Alexa, add [event] to my calendar for [day] at [time]" - Adds an event to your calendar

"Alexa, what's on for today" – Checks your calendar for today

"Alexa, what's my mission" – Checks your calendar

News and weather

"Alexa, what's in the news?" – Checks your news headlines

"Alexa, what's the weather like?" – Checks the weather forecast

"Alexa, what's the weather going to be like on [day]? – Checks the weather forecast for a given day

"Alexa, what's traffic like?" – Gets traffic updates

"Alexa, did the [team] win?" – Gets sport results

"Alexa, what's my Flash Briefing?" – Alexa will give you your flash briefing from the news sources you follow

"Alexa, give me my Sports Update." – Updates you on your preferred sports teams

Media

"Alexa, play some music." – Starts music playback with the default music service

"Alexa, play music by [artist]." – Plays songs by the specified artist

"Alexa, what's playing?" – Tells you what's currently playing

"Alexa, play" – Starts music playback

"Alexa, next." – Skips to the next song

"Alexa, restart." – Restarts a song

"Alexa, loop" – Loops the current song

"Alexa, stop playing in [##] minutes." – Alexa will stop playback after the specified number of minutes

"Alexa, play [title] on Audible – Plays an audiobook from Audible

"Alexa, resume my book." – Resumes last played audio book

"Alexa, next chapter" – Skips to the next chapter in an audio book

"Alexa, previous chapter." – Goes to the previous audiobook chapter

"Alexa, read me my Kindle book." – Alexa reads your kindle book to you

Amazon

"Alexa, reorder [item]." – Reorders a previously purchased item

"Alexa, track my order." – Tracks your Amazon orders

"Alexa, order an Echo," – Orders an Amazon Echo

"Alexa, add [item] to my cart." – Adds an item to your Amazon cart

"Alexa, what are your deals?" – Finds current Amazon deals

Local information

"Alexa, what movies are playing?" – Finds movies playing nearby

"Alexa, what action movies are playing tonight?" – Finds action movies playing nearby at the specified time

"Alexa, find me a nearby pizza restaurant." – Finds local businesses

"Alexa, find the address for [local business]" – Alexa can find addresses, phone numbers and operating hours

General Questions

"Alexa, Wikipedia: [subject]." – Alexa reads the first paragraph of the specified Wikipedia article

"Alexa, tell me more." – Alexa will continue reading the Wikipedia article

"Alexa, [general question] – Alexa can find the answer to most general questions

Chapter 5:

Playing music on your Echo Dot

Alexa supports a number of music streaming services for playback on your Echo Dot. These include Amazon Music, Prime Music, Spotify, Pandora, TuneIn and iHeartRadio. You can also playback music stored on a Bluetooth enabled device such as your mobile phone on your Echo Dot.

Playing music from Amazon Music or Prime music

If you have purchased music from Amazon music, these songs will automatically be available on your Echo Dot as will any music you have uploaded to "My Music" on Amazon. If you are an Amazon Prime member you also have access to Prime music playlists, radio stations and any songs in the Prime music library. To get started listening to your music you can just say "Alexa, play some music".

If you want to play music from Prime music, you'll need to specify this to Alexa by saying "Alexa, play some Prime music". You can also specify what you'd like Alexa to play by saying "Play [song / album / artist] from Prime Music." To stop music playback just say "Alexa, stop". Alexa understands playback commands for "Next", "Previous", "Shuffle", "Loop" and "Repeat".

You can get Alexa to give you details of your currently playing music by asking one of the following questions:

"Alexa, what is this?"

"Alexa, who is this?"

"Alexa, what song is this?"

"Alexa, who is this artist?"

"Alexa, when did this song/album come out?"

Playing music from a third-party music streaming service

If you'd like to use a third-party music provider such as Pandora or Spotify you will need to do some additional setup to link your accounts to your Echo Dot. You can do this by:

1. Open the Alexa app and select "Settings".

2. Select "Music & Media", and then choose which music provider you'd like to link to.

3. Select "Link account to Alexa". A sign-in page will appear.

4. Enter your details to sign in to your account.

Your accounts are now linked and you can play music from your third-party music provider on your Echo Dot. When asking Alexa to play music you will need to specify where you wish to play music from. Here are some sample commands:

"Alexa, play my [artist / genre] station on [Prime Music/ Pandora / iHeartRadio]."

"Alexa, play [title] from Spotify."

"Alexa, play the station [name]."

"Play the podcast [title]."

"Alexa, create an [iHeartRadio / Pandora] station based on [artist]."

Playing music via Bluetooth

To play music via Bluetooth you need to connect your Bluetooth enabled device such as your phone to your Echo Dot. You can do this by:

1. Open the Alexa app and then select "Settings".

2. Select your Echo Dot from the list

3. Select "Bluetooth" > "Pair a New Device". Your Echo Dot enters pairing mode.

4. Open the Bluetooth settings menu on your phone and select your Echo Dot from the device list. Check the user guide for your phone if you are unsure how to do this.

5. Alexa will tell you that connection was successful.

Chapter 5: Playing music on your Echo Dot

Your phone is now connected to your Echo Dot. When you wish to disconnect your phone just say "Alexa, disconnect". You will not need to follow this setup process next time you wish to connect your phone. Just enable Bluetooth on your phone and say "Alexa, connect" to connect your phone again.

You cannot use Alexa voice commands to control playback of music via Bluetooth. You will need to queue up whichever songs you wish to play using your phone and these will play through the speakers connected to your Echo Dot.

Chapter 6:

Other uses for your Echo Dot

Your Echo Dot can do more than just play music. Make the most of the built-in features by using the timer while you cook, the calendar and to-list to keep you organized and the weather function to help choose your outfit of a morning. You can get a lot of use out of your Echo Dot without ever once using it to play music!

Alexa can answer almost any question you have and can even look up Wikipedia or find local business information using Yelp. I've listed some basic commands in chapter 4 and now's a great time to put some of them into use. I recommend you spend a few days getting acquainted with these commands. Try to use a new function each day so you don't get overwhelmed. The next chapter will cover how you can add some more commands to Alexa, so try to brainstorm some ideas of features you'd find helpful.

One of the most popular things you can do with your Echo Dot is use it to control your smart home. You can connect smart devices such as lights or your thermostat to your Echo Dot and then control them by giving voice commands to Alexa. Here are a few beginner friendly recommendations for compatible smart devices:

Philips Hue White Starter Kit

This kit is a great way to get started with using smart lights with your Echo Dot. This kit comes with 2 soft, white LED lights, and also a Hue Hub. A Hue Hub is necessary to connect Hue lights to your Echo Dot, and each hub can connect up to 50 lights so you can keep adding lights as you make your home smarter. The lights included in this kit are basic white lights without any fancy features, but if all you want to be able to do is turn your lights off and on they are perfect. I'm a fan of Phillips Hue lights because they have a huge range of lighting and are easy to set up.

Belkin WeMo Switch & Belkin WeMo Insight Switch

Want to make a dumb appliance smart? The easiest way to do this is to use a smart outlet that will power up your appliance on demand. These plugs allow you to plug in an appliance and turn it off and on by giving a voice command to Alexa. The WeMo Insight Switch is the pricier option of the two, but it adds the ability to track electricity usage.

Nest Learning Thermostat

This is an Amazon best seller and it's no surprise why. It's a modern and sleek looking thermostat and it boasts an impressive list of features. If you're looking to save money on your electricity bill, you might find a smart thermostat a good solution. The Nest Learning Thermostat has the ability to track electricity usage, and also has a feature to automatically adjust the temperature when no one is home so that electricity is not wasted heating or cooling an empty house.

Chapter 7:

Adding more skills to your Echo Dot

Have you got the hang of using some basic commands with your Echo Dot? Do you want to add some more features?

Adding more features to your Echo Dot is easy. You add features by adding "Skills". You can think of a skill as an app that Alexa can run. There are lots of different skills that have been created by third party developers to add functionality to Alexa, and best of all they're free to enable on Alexa for use on your Echo Dot!

There are a few different ways you can add skills to Alexa. If you already know the exact name of the skill you would like to add you could say "Alexa, enable [skill name] skill". Please note that if a skill requires you to link an account such as with Fitbit or Uber you won't be able to enable it by voice.

If you don't know the exact name of a skill you would like to add or you need to link an account, you can use the Alexa app or the Alexa skills store on Amazon to add a skill.

Chapter 7: Adding more skills to your Echo Dot

To enable a skill in the Alexa app:

- From the left navigation panel, select "Skills".

- Use the search bar to enter keywords or select "Categories" to browse through skill categories.

- When you see a skill you want to use, select "Enable Skill".

To enable a skill using the Alexa skills store:

- Browse to https://www.amazon.com/skills on your computer

- Use the search bar to enter keywords or select a category on the left side of the screen to browse through skill categories.

- Select a skill you'd like to enable

- Click "Enable Skill"

To use a skill you've enabled within Alexa, you need to use the skill invocation name. For example, you could say "Alexa, open Uber" or "Alexa, ask Uber to request a ride" to use the Uber skill. In this case "Uber" is the skill invocation name. The invocation name for each skill is unique, and it's not always the same as the skill name itself. It can get confusing to remember a lot of skill invocation names, but if you forget the invocation name for a skill, then you can look up the skill details again using the Alexa app.

If you ever need help with a skill or aren't sure what commands you can use, you can say, "Alexa, help with [skill name] and Alexa will give you some assistance. You can also look at the skill details within the Alexa app for information.

If you no longer wish to use a particular Alexa skill, you can disable it by saying "Alexa, disable [skill name] skill" or you can disable it within the Alexa app by doing the following:

- From the left navigation panel, select "Skills".

- Use the search bar to find the skill you wish to disable

- When you find the skill you want to disable, select "Disable Skill".

Smart Home skills

So how do you get your smart devices set up with Alexa? For most devices this should be simple. Firstly, follow the instructions that came with your smart device to get it set up on your Wi-Fi network. Setup will vary depending on your device – contact the device manufacturer if you're unsure of what to do.

Once your device is connected to your Wi-Fi, you're ready to connect it to Alexa by installing the relevant skill. You can find home automation skills by doing the following:

- In the Alexa app select the "**Menu**" icon (this looks like 3 horizontal lines)

- Select "**Smart Home**".

- Select "**Get More Smart Home Skills**".

- Browse or search keywords for the skill for your smart home device and select "**Enable Skill**".

- If prompted, sign in with your third-party information and then follow the prompts to complete setup.

Not all smart devices will need a skill to allow them to be discovered. These include some Phillips Hue and Belkin WeMo devices. To connect these devices just say "Alexa, discover devices".

Chapter 8:

Recommended Skills

The Alexa app store is growing fast with over 4,000 awesome skills that can be activated using your voice with your Echo Dot!

Earlier in the book, we covered how to add more skills to your Echo Dot. In this chapter we will be giving you some recommendations for the best, most useful, and also funny skills that you'll want to consider enabling.

Here are our top suggestions that you might want to check out in the Alexa Skills store.

Fitbit

If you own and use a Fitbit, you'll be happy to hear that it can now integrate with Alexa on all Alexa enabled devices!

This allows you to get fast updates on a variety of different stats, such as steps taken, exercise goals, and sleep information.

The downsides are that it doesn't work with multiple Fitbit accounts, and is still quite basic in its functions.

7-Minute Workout

Another exercise skill, the 7-Minute workout allows you to try a variety of different short workouts, and track your progress as you do so!

This skill allows you to perform a quick, 7-minute, fat-burning workout with the help of your Echo, Echo Dot, or Amazon Tap. Even better, you can perform the workout whilst wearing a Fitbit to have even more data recorded by Alexa!

Stock Exchange

The Stock Exchange skill allows you to keep an eye on the performance of your portfolio, as well as gather information about the market.

Currently, Alexa can provide you information about a range of stocks. Unfortunately, Alexa often misunderstands you with this skill when asking about certain stocks, and subsequently provides the wrong information.

CryptoCurrency

This skill lets you instantly check the prices of Bitcoin. If you trade Bitcoin, this simple skill can be handy for tracking the market value more quickly than before.

Capital One

The Capital One skill allows you to check your bank transactions, balance, and pay bills, all using voice commands.

This is a very useful skill, though you do need to be cautious of the obvious security threats that using this may pose.

Mortgage Calculator

This skill may sound boring, but it's very practical. It allows you to calculate monthly payments based on your principal amount, loan length, and interest rate.

Yo Momma Jokes

A silly skill, Yo Momma Jokes will tell you a whole heap of different jokes that will appeal to most. However, it doesn't have an age setting and so some of the jokes might not be suitable for the whole family!

4A Fart

Possibly the silliest skill in the store is the 4A Fart skill. As you might have guessed, this skill allows Alexa to make fart noises on command. Simple, but funny.

Pickup Lines

A funny skill for the guys to use, Pickup Lines will cause Alexa to fire off some dirty one-liners. Not only that, she also interjects in-between pickup lines with some funny comments, giving her more personality than you'll see in almost all other skills.

SmartThings

If you want to create a smart home, then the SmartThings skill is what you're looking for. This allows Alexa to perform a range of functions within your home, such as controlling lights, thermostats, and security systems.

However, this skill does require that you also purchase a SmartThings hub, and some of the equipment such as lights and security components can be quite expensive.

Mosaic

Mosaic is a skill that allows you to control your Hue lights, Nest Learning Thermostat, and even your Tesla car! It allows you to perform functions such as dimming lights, and changing the temperature of your house.

The downside however is that the required components such as compatible lights and thermostat will come at an additional cost.

Automatic

The Automatic skill lets you sync Alexa with your car. It can provide information such as car location, gas, and the distance you have driven!

It does however require an Automatic account and adapter, which will come at an additional cost.

The Magic Door

A great skill for children, The Magic Door allows you to create your own story. Using the skill, you can choose up to three different story settings, and each choice you make will alter the outcome of the tale. It takes story telling to a whole new place, making it an interactive activity.

Right now however, the stories are quite short and there are only a limited number available. As time goes on though, you should expect more to be added.

Akinator

The Akinator skill is essentially Alexa's version of '20 questions'.

You simply think of an object, and Alexa will begin questioning you to find out what it is. Make sure to answer clear though, otherwise the skill won't work to its full potential.

Amazing Word Master Game

This skill is one of the best games for Alexa so far!

Alexa starts by saying a word, to which you have to respond with a word that begins with the letter that Alexa's ended with.

This continues on and on, and you receive points based on the length of the words you say. The game goes on until someone fails to respond, or you choose to end the game.

Overall, it's a fun and mentally stimulating game to play on your own, or with friends.

The Wayne Investigation

This skill is a fun, Batman adventure game.

Similar to The Magic Door skill, you get to interact with the story and make choices along the way. This one is Batman themed, and has a variety of different stories and options to choose from.

The audio is really high quality, and this is easily one of the best game skills currently available!

Jeopardy

Just like the TV show, the Jeopardy skill will fire off questions for you to answer. This helps you to build your general knowledge, and can be a fun way to challenge friends!

Trainer Tips

For the Pokemon lovers out there, Trainer Tips will help you to increase your Pokémon knowledge! This skill can spout out random Pokémon facts, and also answer specific questions about the Pokémon you want to learn about.

Potterhead Quiz

The Potterhead Quiz is a simple skill that will fire off questions about the world of Harry Potter. Test your Potter knowledge against your friends with this fun skill.

TV Shows

TV Shows allows you to ask Alexa when your favorite shows are playing. Be sure to be clear with your commands though, as this skill can sometimes get mixed up between different shows if you don't speak clearly!

Uber

The Uber skill works similarly to the app, and lets you request an Uber using your voice. It can also provide you information on the ride options and status, and can even be used to cancel the Uber.

Lyft

Uber's main competitor, Lyft, also has a skill available. It works in the same way, allowing you to order a Lyft using a simple voice command.

In addition, you can enquire about Lyft's pricing by asking things like "Alexa, ask Lyft how much a Lyft Plus will cost from home to work".

1-800-Flowers

This skill makes gift giving easy, and allows you to send flowers through a simple voice command!

You can choose from a variety of floral arrangements, and set a delivery date of your choice. Prior to using this skill, you will need to create a 1-800 Flowers account, and then sync it up.

The only real negative to this skill is that it currently doesn't have as wide of a selection as you can get from the online version.

WineMate

The WineMate skill helps you to choose the perfect wine to pair with your food. Simply enable the skill, and then ask Alexa what wine would go well with (XYZ) food! It works in the opposite way too, meaning you can ask Alexa which food would go well with your chosen wine.

What Beer

Just like the WineMate skill, What Beer helps you to choose which beer you should have with your meal.

The Bartender

The Bartender is a fun skill that provides you with recipes for your favorite cocktails! In an instant, Alexa will tell you the different ingredients you need for your desired cocktail, and will even give you drink suggestions.

Campbell's Kitchen

The Campbell's Kitchen skill is an extension of the well-known recipe app of the same name.

In an instant, Alexa will be able to give you recipes for a huge selection of meals. It can also be used to send you an e-mail or app summary showing the recipes you've chosen.

QuickBits

Another food skill, QuickBits is designed for those who don't have much time to spend in the kitchen. This skill provides you with a ton of different recipes that can all be made in 10-minutes or less!

All you have to do is ask QuickBits how to make your favorite fast meal, and Alexa will respond with the recipe!

Meat Thermometer

Another food-related skill, Meat Thermometer tells you the correct internal temperature you should bring your meat to when cooking. It has information on a range of different meats, and is a simple way to improve your cooking!

Food Finder

This cool skill will let you know where you can find food in your area. Simply tell the skill "I want Thai food in (insert zip code)" and it will let you know the available places!

It works with all different food types, and saves you searching through web results to find a suitable place.

Domino's Pizza

A simple but awesome skill, this allows you to be even lazier when ordering pizza. Now you don't even need to move, and can order from Dominos with just a voice command!

You can also track your order status with this skill, and it even remembers your recent orders, and your favorites list. This one is currently only available in the US, but it's likely it will become available elsewhere soon!

Kayak

Kayak is a great travel skill that helps you to research prices for future trips. Simply ask Alexa where you can travel to for '$X', or enquire about flight prices for certain dates.

Kayak will search the web, and give you the different price options for trips instantly.

Guitar Tuner

If you're a guitar player, you definitely want to download this skill!

It simply plays the guitar notes from the low E string, up to the high E string, so you can tune your guitar by ear.

HuffPost

The HuffPost skill will read out the headlines from the Huffington Post so that you can get a quick idea of what's happening in the news, and what you might like to read about.

1 Minute Mindfulness

This skill lets you enter a 1-minute sound meditation. If you're feeling stressed out and need a quick break, you can enable this skill to begin meditating right away.

You can select different styles of meditation too, such as a forest meditation, or a beach meditation.

Twitter

The official Twitter skill will read out tweets from your timeline, find trending topics, and read out tweets that you have liked in the past.

If you don't want to pick up your phone to find out what's been said recently on Twitter, then just say "Alexa, ask Twitter what's happening".

Ask My Buddy

This skill is great for people with disabilities, as it allows you to send a distress signal to friends and family. If you need help, or in the case of an accident or emergency, you can use this skill to send distress messages to one, or all, of your chosen contacts.

Chapter 9:

50 Fun things to Ask Alexa

Besides using your Echo Dot for practical purposes, you can also have a bit of fun with it too! The following questions and comments will all get a witty response from Alexa that is sure to keep you entertained!

1. Alexa, how old is Santa Claus?

2. Alexa, can I tell you a secret?

3. Alexa, what's the magic word?

4. Alexa, do you smoke?

5. Alexa, are you smoking?

6. Alexa, what is your favorite food?

7. Alexa, what is your favorite drink?

8. Alexa, are you hungry/thirsty?

9. Alexa, what is your feature?

10. Alexa, do you have any pets?

11. Alexa, who is your best friend?

12. Alexa, what religion are you?

13. Alexa, are you God?

14. Alexa, are you evil?

15. Alexa, what language do you speak?

16. Alexa, am I funny?

17. Alexa, can I tell you a joke?

18. Alexa, what is happiness?

19. Alexa, what size shoe do you wear?

20. Alexa, what makes you happy?

21. Alexa, who's on first?

22. Alexa, fire photon torpedos.

23. Alexa, live long and prosper.

24. Alexa, open the pod bay doors.

25. Alexa, these aren't the droids you're looking for.

26. Alexa, take me to your leader.

27. Alexa, does this unit have a soul?

28. Alexa, do you like green eggs and ham?

29. Alexa, one fish, two fish.

30. Alexa, what was the Lorax?

31. Alexa, why do you sit there like that?

32. Alexa, why do birds suddenly appear?

33. Alexa, to be or not to be.

34. Alexa, beam me up.

35. Alexa, I am your father.

36. Alexa, may the force be with you.

37. Alexa, Tea. Earl Grey. Hot.

38. Alexa, Warp 10

39. Alexa, party time!

40. Alexa, are you working?

41. Alexa, heads or tails?

42. Alexa, random number between "x" and "y".

43. Alexa, what number are you thinking of?

44. Alexa, count by ten.

45. Alexa, rock, paper, scissors.

46. Alexa, random fact

47. Alexa, what is the meaning of life?

48. Alexa, when is the end of the world?

49. Alexa, when am I going to die?

50. Alexa, what is the airspeed velocity of an unladen swallow?

Chapter 10:

Troubleshooting and FAQ

I'm concerned for my privacy; how can I stop Alexa from listening to my conversations?

You can mute the microphone of your Echo Dot. The mute button is located on the top of the Echo Dot, and looks like a microphone with a slash through it. The light ring on your device will glow red when the microphone is muted and you will not be able to wake Alexa with the wake word. To resume using Alexa, unmute your microphone by pressing the mute button again.

I'd like to delete the recordings Alexa has taken of my voice.

Alexa records some of your queries to improve her recognition of your voice. If you delete these recordings, Alexa may not be as accurate at recognizing the questions you ask her. If you still wish to delete these recordings, you can do so by taking the following steps:

1. Open the Alexa app.

2. Select "**Settings**" in the navigation panel of the left

3. Select "**History**".

4. Select a recording from the list

5. Select the "**Play**" icon to listen to the recording if you wish to.

6. Select "**Delete voice recording**"

The light ring is orange and spinning clockwise. What is happening?

Your Echo Dot is attempting to connect to Wi-Fi. If this happens often it indicates that your Echo Dot is receiving a weak Wi-Fi signal and may be too far away from your router. You should try moving your Echo Dot closer to your router. This could also indicate that your network is congested or something is interfering with your Wi-Fi network. To combat this, you can try reducing the number of devices that are connected to your network or try moving your Echo Dot away from potential sources of interference such as microwaves and baby monitors.

If none of the above helps the issue, you can try restarting your Echo Dot and your router. This will resolve most intermittent Wi-Fi issues.

1. Turn off your router, and then wait 30 seconds. Ask your router manufacturer or Internet service provider if you are unsure how to do this.

2. Turn on your router and then wait for it to restart. You will usually have some status lights to indicate when this process is complete.

3. While your network hardware restarts, unplug the power adapter from your Echo Dot for three seconds, and then plug it back in.

4. Once your Echo Dot and router have restarted, attempt to connect to Wi-Fi again.

The light ring is violet and flashing. What is wrong?

This indicates that something went wrong during Wi-Fi setup. The first thing you should do is attempt the Wi-Fi setup again. Make sure you are connecting to the right network and that you are entering your network password if one is required. Ensure that your password and other details are correct.

You should check that other devices such as your laptop or mobile phone are able to connect to the network. If they cannot, this indicates that there is a problem with your network. You may need to contact your Internet service provider for help with troubleshooting network problems.

If you had previously saved your Wi-Fi password within the Alexa app, you may need to update your password within the Alexa app if it has changed recently.

If none of the above helps the issue, you can try restarting your Echo Dot and your router. This will resolve most intermittent Wi-Fi issues.

1. Turn off your router, and then wait 30 seconds. Ask your router manufacturer or Internet service provider if you are unsure how to do this.

2. Turn on your router and then wait for it to restart. You will usually have some status lights to indicate when this process is complete.

3. While your network hardware restarts, unplug the power adapter from your Echo Dot for three seconds, and then plug it back in.

4. Once your Echo Dot and router have restarted, attempt to connect to Wi-Fi again.

As a last resort you may need to contact your router manufacturer or Internet service provider for assistance.

Alexa has trouble understanding me. What can I do?

You can do voice training to improve how well Alexa understands your voice. Within the Alexa app select "Settings" and then "Voice Training". Alexa will now have you repeat some phrases to improve her voice recognition.

If this doesn't resolve the issue, you may need to move your Echo Dot to a better location. It is recommended that your Echo Dot is at least 8-inches away from walls or other objects, and it is not placed on the floor. You should also try to reduce the amount of background noise in your environment and speak loudly and clearly to Alexa.

Alexa is activating accidentally. How can I prevent this?

If you find Alexa is being activated accidentally you can change the wake word of your device. You can choose from either "Alexa", "Amazon" or "Echo" for the wake word.

1. In the Alexa app, select the menu icon. This looks like three horizontal lines.

2. Select "Settings"

3. Select your device

4. Select "Wake word"

5. Select your preferred wake word from the drop down menu

If you find that this issue only occurs intermittently when the environment is noisy, such as when you are hosting a party, you can temporarily mute the microphones on your Echo Dot rather than changing the wake word. The mute button is located on the top of your Echo Dot and resembles a microphone with a slash through it. The light ring on your Echo Dot will glow red when your microphone is muted. You can press the mute button again to unmute your microphones.

How do I pair Bluetooth devices?

You can pair Bluetooth devices by doing the following:

1. Set your mobile device to Bluetooth pairing mode and ensure you are in range of your device.

2. Say, "Alexa, Pair." Alexa will notify you that your device is ready to pair.

3. Open Bluetooth settings on your mobile device and select to pair with your Echo Dot. Alexa will notify you if pairing is successful.

4. If you are unable to connect, you can exit Bluetooth mode by saying "Alexa, Cancel"

5. When you wish to disconnect your mobile device you can say "Alexa, disconnect"

Once your Echo Dot has been paired you will not have to repeat this process. In future when you want to connect to a previously paired device you can say "Alexa, connect."

I can't get my smart devices set up. What is wrong?

Make sure your smart device is compatible with Alexa. The list of compatible devices changes frequently, so check with Amazon if you are unsure. If your device is incompatible with Alexa, you may still by able to use it through the use of If This Then That (IFTTT). IFTTT is a free home automation service that has native support on Amazon Alexa. You can find more details at https://ifttt.com

If your device is compatible with Alexa, make sure it is set up correctly on your local Wi-Fi network. You may have to download an app from your device manufacturer to get your smart device set up correctly. If you can change the name of your smart device through the manufacturers app, ensure that the name can be understood by Alexa. Stick to simple words and avoid numbers or punctuation. If you're unsure how to get your smart device set up, you should check with the device manufacturer.

If your device is set up correctly on your Wi-Fi network but you are still unable to connect, you may need to restart both your smart device and your Amazon device. Check the user manual of your smart device for instructions on how to turn it off and on again. You can also try disabling and re-enabling the skill for your device within the Alexa app. This should fix most problems.

If you have Phillips or WeMo devices, you will not need to enable a skill to discover these devices. To enable these devices, you can simply say "Alexa, discover devices".

How can I use the US/UK/Germany Alexa skills store?

To use a different version of the Alexa skills store you will need an Amazon account for that locality. You will need to reset your Echo Dot and then follow the instructions for setting up your Echo Dot with this Amazon account. Resetting your Echo Dot will erase all of your settings and return it to the same state it was in when you first bought it.

To reset your Echo Dot:

1. Use a paper clip (or similar tool) to press and hold the "**Reset**" button for five seconds. The reset button is located on the base of your Echo Dot.

2. The light ring will turn orange and then blue. Wait for the light ring to turn off and then back on again. Once the light ring is glowing solid orange, your device is in setup mode.

3. You can now proceed to setup your Echo Dot.

Conclusion

Thanks again for taking the time to read this book!

You should now know how to use your Echo Dot quite comfortably, and be able to confidently use it for a ton of different uses!

If you enjoyed this book, please take the time to leave me a review on Amazon. I appreciate your honest feedback, and it really helps me to continue producing high quality books.